OTAKAR ŠEVČÍK Op. 16, No. 44

Paganini - Moses Fantasy Variations
Complete Violin & Piano Score
Critical Urtext Violin Part

Analytical Studies & Exercises

Edited by Stephen Shipps

KEISER

PREFACE

Italian virtuoso violinist and composer NICCOLO PAGANINI was born in Genoa in 1782. His early training consisted of lessons with his father and local teachers in Genoa. He moved to Parma to continue his training with Alessandro Rolla, but his innate performing gifts quickly outpaced all teachers and mentors. As a young teenager he commenced on a course of his own study that was so intense that he eclipsed all preceding violinists in history. It is an important note that this great virtuosity was almost completely self-taught, a remarkable historical accomplishment.

In 1797 he began his life of concert tours in Italy which was immediately successful. In 1801, he became the First Violinist of Republic of Lucca. When Lucca was conquered by Napoleon in 1802, Paganini's title was transferred with his being named the Court Violinist to Elisa Baciocchi, the sister of Napoleon. Baciocchi became the Grand Duchess of Tuscany soon thereafter and Paganini remained as part of her royal entourage until 1809.

From this point on in Paganini's life, he reigned as the greatest violinist in the world. He began by touring in Italy and then built his career to appear in all of the great capitals of Europe. His rivals were the two greatest violinists of that time, Louis Spohr and Henri Lafont, however, both of their careers have become small footnotes in history as Paganini has retained his position of eminence. Paganini's life as a composer began as a very young man and continued throughout his entire career as the great bulk of his performing repertoire were his own compositions. The most famous of his compositions are the **Caprices, op. 1** and the six **Concerti**, however, Paganini constantly toured with smaller pieces that he performed with orchestra or piano. These pieces include the *Variations on Nel Cor Piu Non Mi Sento, I Palpiti, Variations on God Save the King, Cantabile* and many others.

The *Variations on a Theme from Rossini's Moses* is one his most famous and often-performed virtuoso display compositions. Being the ultimate showman and almost circus performer, Paganini prided himself in compositions completely beyond the capabilities of the other violinists of his day. Paganini would often play final pieces in his programs on a single string, often also using the technical effect of *scordatura*, or retuning the instrument. One of his most famous concert pyrotechnics was to break the three upper strings in the concert and finish the concert with one piece performed on the G string of the violin. The most famous of these compositions was the *Moses Fantasia* composed as a theme and variations from Rossini's **Moses in Egypt**. Paganini played this composition with the G string tuned up a minor third to the pitch of Bb. The editors have included two separate piano parts so as to provide the option for the performer to use normal tuning or Paganini's original *scordatura.*

In a curious historical note, no manuscript exists, as Paganini did not want any other virtuoso to steal this work. It was published posthumously and immediately became a sensation in the 19th century. It is currently not only performed on the violin but has been transcribed for the cello and double bass. We are proud to bring this version based on the earlier published version supplemented by the marvelous exercises written by Otakar Ševčík in the 1920's.

Stephen Shipps

Variazioni de Bravura Sulla Quarta Corda

sopra temi del MOSÈ di G. Rossini
for
Violin and Piano

NICCOLO PAGANINI
edited by Stephen Shipps

16
19
23
mf
27
rit.
p
dim.
6
pp
f
rit.

30
a tempo
Maggiore
a tempo
34
38
42
cadenza

Thema

Var. I
p
f
rit.
f
a tempo
p
rit.
a tempo
p
mf
5
cresc.
f
rit.
a tempo
f
cresc.
rit.
a tempo
f
9
p
cresc.
f
rit.
f
p
p
mf
rit.
14
a tempo
f
rit.
a tempo
f
a tempo
p
rit.
a tempo
f

Var. II
9
cresc.
rit.
a tempo
rit.
17
rit.
a tempo
rit.
cresc.
a tempo
rit.
a tempo
rit.
24
rit.
a tempo
rit.
a tempo
30
1.
2.
1.
2.

Var. III
f repeat ponticello
p
7
naturale
f
pp
13
ponticello
a tempo
19
rit.
a tempo
naturale

25
cresc.
f
cresc.
cresc.
30
ff
f
35
f
segue
mf
40
cresc.
ff
cresc.
ff

OTAKAR ŠEVČÍK Op. 16, No. 44

Paganini - Moses Fantasy Variations

Critical Edition Violin Part

Analytical Studies & Exercises

(Ševčík Studies Op. 16, No. 44 begin on page 6)

Edited by Stephen Shipps

KEISER®

OTAKAR ŠEVČÍK STUDIES OP. 16, NO. 44
ABBREVIATIONS AND SIGNS

	Designation of the Length of the Bow by means of fractions:
$\frac{1}{1}$ $\frac{1}{2}$	Whole, half Bow
$\frac{1.}{2}$ $\frac{2.}{2}$	First, second Half
$\frac{1}{3}$ $\frac{2}{3}$	One, two Third
$\frac{1.}{3}$ $\frac{2.}{3}$ $\frac{3.}{3}$	First, second, third Third
$\frac{1}{4}$ $\frac{3}{4}$	One, three Quarters
$\frac{1.}{4}$ $\frac{2.}{4}$ $\frac{3.}{4}$ $\frac{4.}{4}$	First, second, third, fourth Quarter
$\frac{2.\ 3.}{4}$	Second and third Quarters
⊓	Down-bow
V	Up-bow [1])
–	Broad-bow
• •	Short, detached (staccato)
▾ ▾	Springing, bounding (sautillé; spiccato; saltato)
ʾ	Lift Bow
(2	Lift the 2nd. Finger
/	Stop (artificial pause) [2])
I II III IV	I first String E, II second String A, III third String D, IV fourth String G
o	Open String
♪	The left hand off the finger board, the bow remaining on the string
sul E	On the E-string
1 ___	First Finger remains on string
└──	The little hook indicates which Finger is to remain on string
tr	Trills
∿∿	Vibrato, Tremolo
pizz.	Pizzicato with the right hand
+	Pizzicato with the left hand
gliss.	Glissando — gliding
M.	Middle of the Bow
Fr.	At the Nut
Sp.	At the Point
◇ (footed)	(footed Square) Harmonic tone
◇	(without Foot) Passive suporting Finger or Transitiontone
2-4 (boxed)	Study for 2.-4. bar from the Solo

[1]) *Unless otherwise indicated, the first measure begins at the nut.*

[2]) *Lift Bow and make a brief pause.*

Violin

Variazioni de Bravura Sulla Quarta Corda

sopra temi del MOSÈ di G. Rossini
for
Violin and Piano

NICCOLO PAGANINI
edited by Stephen Shipps

Violin

Thema
Tempo alla marcia
rit.
a tempo
cresc.
ossia (8va)
Var. I
sim.
Var. II

Violin

rit.
a tempo
rit.
a tempo
cresc.
Var. III
repeat ponticello
naturale
ponticello
a tempo
rit.
a tempo
naturale
cresc.
segue

44.

N. PAGANINI, MOSES-FANTASIE.
EXERCISES

Passages between two double bar lines are to be repeated several times.

Introduction.

In eighth notes with 11 styles of bowing.

Interv.-Cadenz.

39 – 52

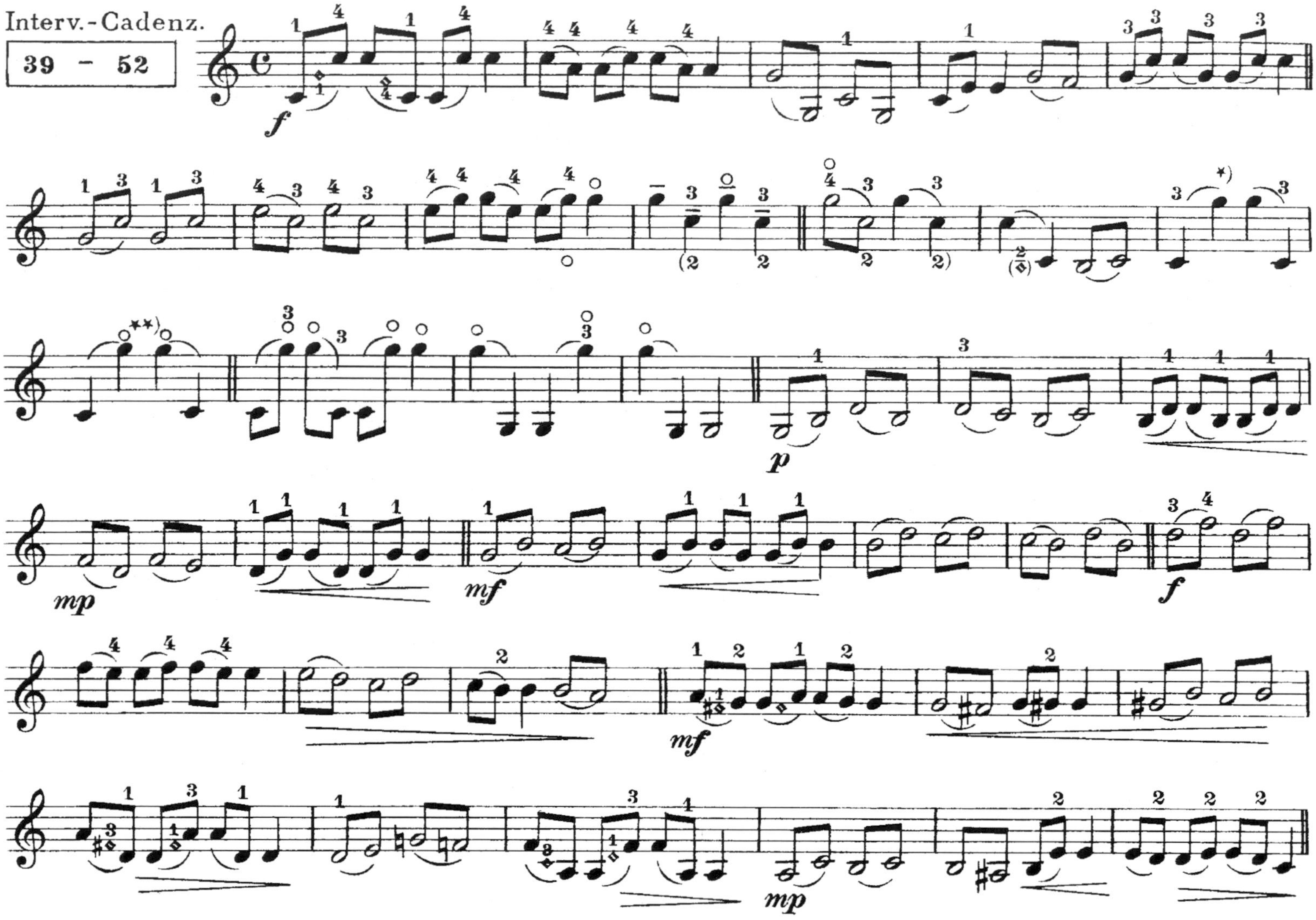

Anal.-Cadenz.

★) without flageolet

★★) While gliding, press the string strongly with the third finger.

Cadenza

with 11 bowing styles

Introduction II

The leading 8 bars of the introduction should be played in flageolets when repeated. To perform those plainly, especially in the high positions, the gliding technique should be practiced as follows. This preparatory study includes bounds in flageolets over 2, 3, 4, and several positions.

From the 5th position to higher positions.

*) from the 4th position.
**) from the 3rd position.
***) from the 2nd position.
+) from the 1st position.
++) from the open string.

Thema.

Passage

with 12 bowings

7 - 8

Analysis

by 5 tones

8 - 12

Passage

with 13 bowings

9 - 12

Variation I.

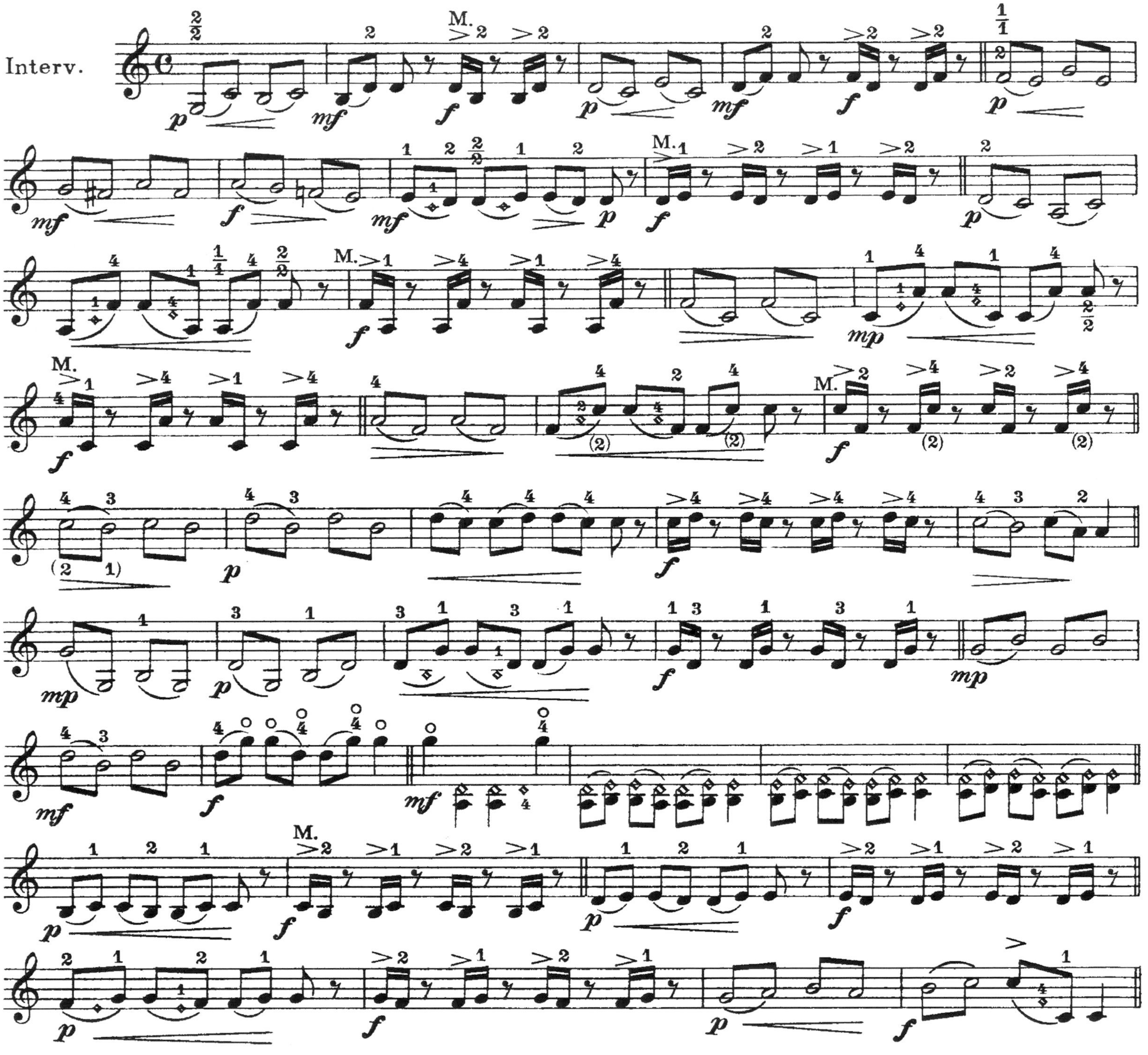

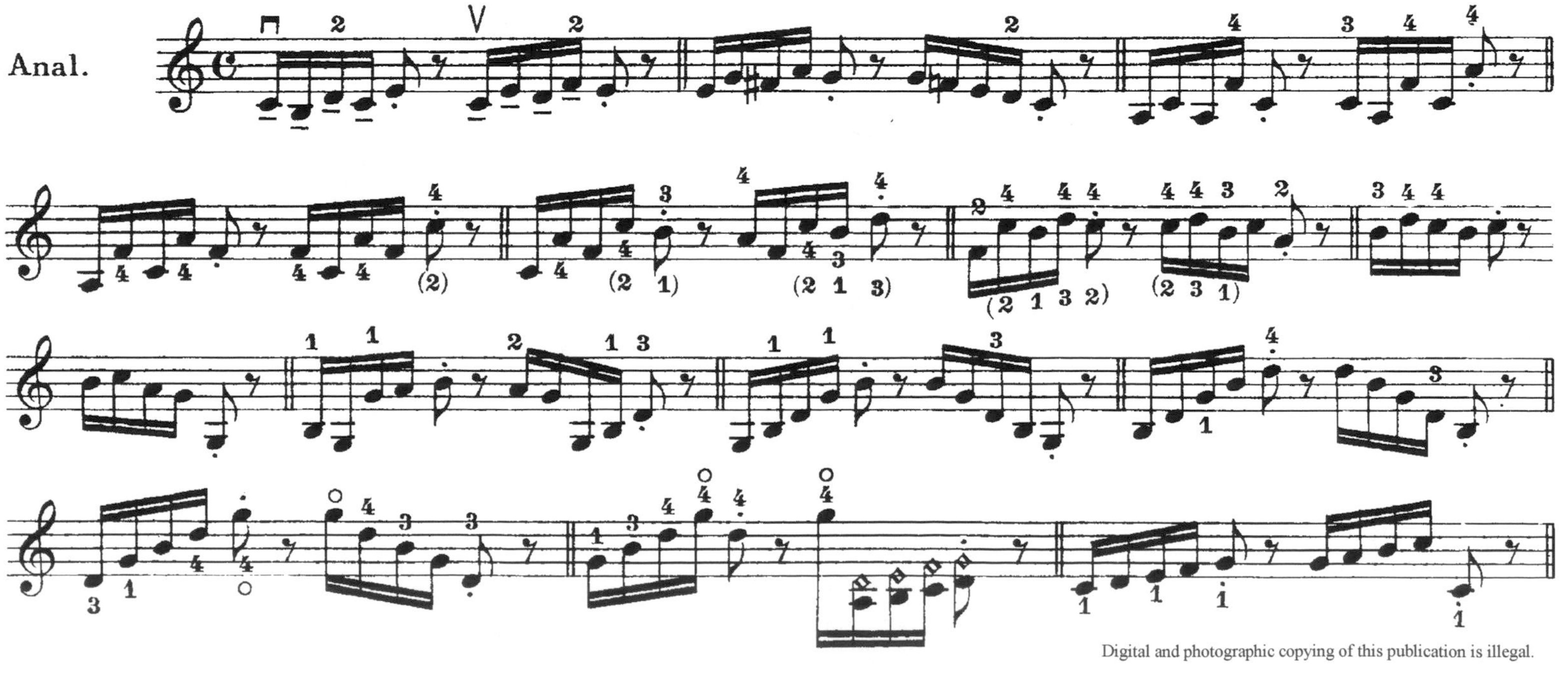

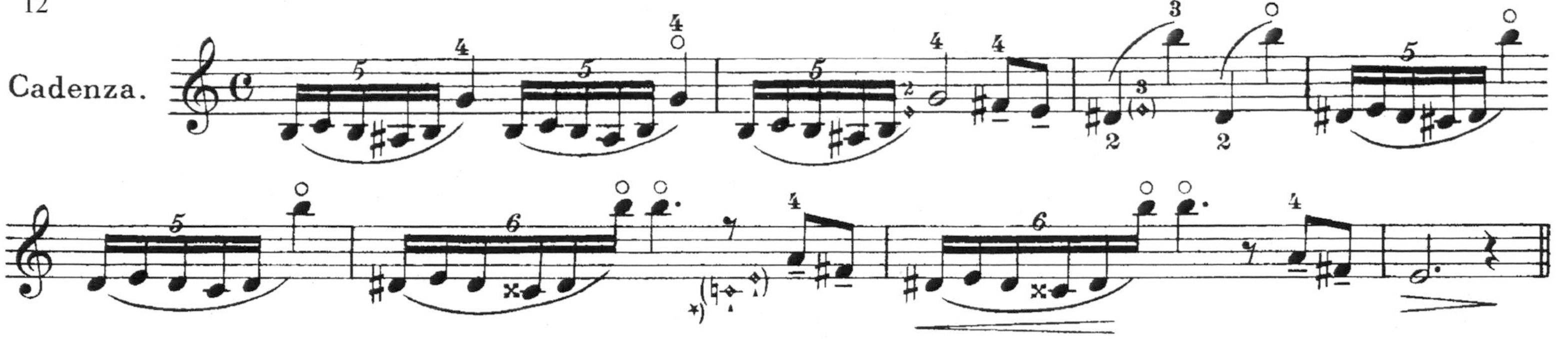

Passage from Variation I

with 20 styles of bowing

Viotti's stroke.

Paganini's stroke.

★) Preparation for the 5th position

Variation II.

Variation III

Paganini's stroke
(Triplet stroke on eighth or sixteenth notes.)

The *ponticello* is to be executed near the bridge with the topmost third of the bow without much pressure (*mp*, *mf*). To remain with the bow near the bridge, angle it a little forward and not parallel with the bridge.

★) Count or tap quarter notes while practicing
★★) The bow should not be lifted

Finale.

Continuation

Continuation.

Finale

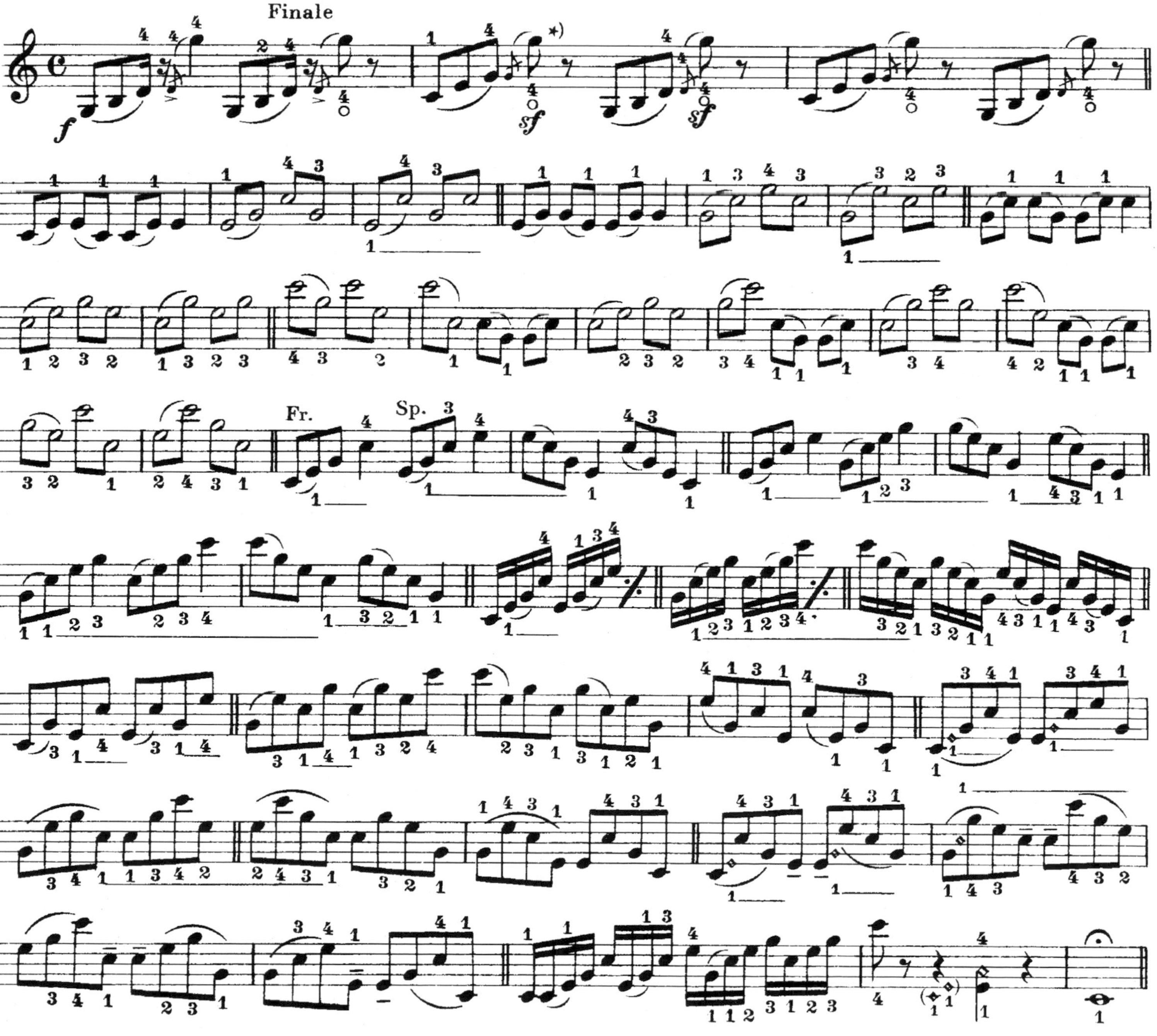

★) When performing the *appogiatura,* the flageolet tone also works well with fast tempi.

Variazioni de Bravura Sulla Quarta Corda

sopra temi del MOSÈ di G. Rossini
for
Violin and Piano

NICCOLO PAGANINI
edited by Stephen Shipps

16
19
23
mf
27
rit.
p
dim.
pp
f
rit.

30
a tempo
Maggiore
a tempo
34
38
42
cadenza

Thema

Tempo alla marcia
rit.
a tempo
Tempo alla marcia
rit.
a tempo
5
rit.
a tempo
cresc.
rit.
a tempo
8
3
13
ossia
rit. (8va)
a tempo
cresc.
rit.
a tempo

Var. I
rit.
a tempo
5
cresc.
rit.
a tempo
9
cresc.
rit.
rit.
14
a tempo
rit.
a tempo
a tempo
rit.
a tempo

Var. II
p
f
p
p
f
9
cresc.
rit.
a tempo
f
p
p
rit.
mf
17
a tempo
p
rit.
f
a tempo
p
rit.
cresc.
24
rit.
a tempo
f
p
f
ppp
30
1.
2.
ff
ff

Var. III
f repeat ponticello
p
7
naturale
f
pp
p
13
ponticello
pp
a tempo
f
a tempo
p
19
p
rit.
a tempo
naturale
6
6
p
rit.
a tempo
p

25
cresc.
cresc.
cresc.
30
35
segue
40
cresc.
cresc.

Otakar Ševčík Series

In 1881, Otakar Ševčík, the 29 year-old newly appointed professor of the Kiev Conservatory, forever changed the way violin technique would be studied with the publication of his Op. 1, Violin Left-Hand Technique. Nearly fifty years after the appearance of this ground-breaking work, Ševčík's pioneering spirit took him in the new direction of writing repertoire-specific exercises. Each edition in the series includes a solo violin part, a piano accompaniment and the Analytical Studies written for the particular piece. After having been out of print for over 75 years, these new publications now makes Ševčík's Analytical Studies available to an entirely new generation of violinists. Accompanying each volume is a modern edition of each selected work by editors Endre Granat and Stephen Shipps.

OTAKAR ŠEVČÍK OP. 16 NO. 40: Wieniawski Scherzo-Tarantelle + Analytical Studies S511012

This edition is based upon years of study with Editor Stephen Shipps' teacher, Josef Gingold. Gingold studied the Scherzo-Tarantelle with Eugène Ysaÿe who in turn studied it directly with the composer, Henryk Wieniawski. Practical suggestions from Wieniawski are marked *ossia* in the violin part. The original manuscript and first edition published by Freidrich Kistner of Leipzig were consulted in making this the first ever edition to combine a modern version of the violin part with the historic and timeless exercises by Ševčík.

OTAKAR ŠEVČÍK OP. 16 NO. 42: Ernst Hungarian Airs + Analytical Studies S511029

Heinrich Wilhelm Ernst was the most famous violinist in the world at the time of Paganini's death. As a composer, he is chiefly known for his virtuoso pieces such as these "Hungarian Airs." His music was in the standard repertoire into the early part of the 20th Century but was forgotten for many decades. With the advent of the cd, the Ernst's compositions have been recorded and have begun re-emerging into the standard repertory. This edition unites a critical urtext violin part by Stephen Shipps with the piano score and Otakar Sevcik exercises specific to this important virtuoso work.

OTAKAR ŠEVČÍK OP. 16 NO. 44: Paganini Moses Fantasy + Analytical Studies.. S511030

The Variations on a Theme from Rossini's Moses is one Niccolo Paganini's most famous and often performed virtuoso display compositions. Being the ultimate showman and almost circus performer, Paganini prided himself in compositions completely beyond the capabilities of the other violinists of his day. He would often play final pieces in his programs on a single string. One of his most famous concert pyrotechnics was to break the three upper strings in the concert and finish the concert with one piece performed on the G string of the violin. The Moses Fantasia, composed as a theme and variations from Rossini's Moses in Egypt, is the best known example of such a piece. We are proud to bring this version based on the earlier published version supplemented by the marvelous exercises written by Ottakar Ševčík in the 1920's.

OTAKAR ŠEVČÍK OP. 17: Wieniawski Concerto in d minor + Analytical Studies S511014

The Violin Concerto in d minor op.22 shows Wieniawski the composer in full maturity. The thematic material ranges from the beautifully lyrical first movement to the fiery *a la Zingara*. The virtuoso violin part is brilliantly written. The composer first presented this concerto in 1862 in St.Petersburg. Though the performance was a rousing success, Wieniawski rewrote and condensed the piece during the next six years. In 1868 he performed the work in its present form. This edition is based on the original orchestra score and violin piano reduction printed in 1870 by Schott in Mainz, Germany.

OTAKAR ŠEVČÍK OP. 18 & 25: Brahms Concerto in D Major + Analytical Studies S511017

Johannes Brahms dedicated his only Violin Concerto to the great Hungarian violinist, Joseph Joachim. Joachim's suggestions have been sought by the composer for creating the solo part. At the same time he wrote a Cadenza that met with Brahms' approval and is perhaps the most often performed cadenza of the Concerto. This edition is the first to unite the critical Urtext versions of the Concerto, the Cadenza by Joachim, and the corresponding Ševčík op. 18 and op. 25 studies.

OTAKAR ŠEVČÍK OP. 19: Tchaikovsky Concerto in D Major + Analytical Studies...................................... S511013

Combines urtext quality solo material with exercises based on renowned 20th-Century violin pedagogue, Otakar Sevcik's, work. The unique aspect of this edition is the Violin part which includes both the original and the Leopold Auer edition. This publication presents the first opportunity for performers to utilize both versions to create their own unique interpretation of this great work.

OTAKAR ŠEVČÍK OP. 20: Paganini Concerto No. 1 in D major + Analytical Studies.................................. S511016

After being out of print for over 75 years, Ševčík's practice guide to Paganini's ultimate display piece for violin and orchestra is available for the first time with this modern and corrected publication. This Urtext edition includes a new violin part prepared from the manuscript with practical applications and suggestions throughout, as well as a corrected cadenza of Emile Sauret, edited by distinguished violin artist and professor Stephen Shipps.

OTAKAR ŠEVČÍK OP. 21: Mendelssohn Concerto in e minor + Analytical Studies....................................... S511011

This critical Urtext edition of Mendelssohn's Violin Concerto is derived from both the original manuscript score and the first published version by Breitkopf and Härtel. The editor has resolved the minor differences between these two sources. This edition reunites the concerto with the accompanying exercises by world renowned pedagogue, Otakar Ševčík, for the first time since its initial publication. These repertoire -specific exercises address each measure of this entire concerto and suggest solutions for its technical difficulties.

THE ESSENTIAL ŠEVČÍK S510008

The Essential Sevcik is a compendium of the finest, most time-saving learning material by Otakar Sevcik ever assembled in a single volume. It is indispensable for building a thorough, virtuoso technique and an important part of the daily practice regimen for the accomplished artist. These exercises are to be practiced with total concentration and attention to the smallest detail. The clear and straight forward organization of this volume will facilitate finding the most suitable practice material for every violinist.

The HEIFETZ *Collection for Violin*

KEISERSOUTHERNMUSIC.COM

Jascha Heifetz is known to be one of the greatest violinsts in the history of music. He appeared on concert stages from 1920 through 1970 throughout the world. His teaching methods have never been published previously, making the Heifetz Collection an important contribution to sharing his legacy with current and future generations of violinists. Our world-class editors Endre Granat and Stephen Shipps have uncovered these hidden treasures, painstakingly producing unique editions worthy of Jascha Heifetz' legendary standards.

NEW - TCHAIKOVSKY: COMPLETE WORKS FOR VIOLIN AND PIANO ed. Endre Granat • This Critical Performance Edition is primarily based on the first print by the Russian publisher Jurgenson. In the *Andante Funebre* and *Humoresque*, the quartet and piano versions, respectively, were used for comparison. The composer accepted corrections by Leopold Auer and Vassily Bezekirsky, which are indicated in the violin part. Mr. Heifetz's enormous repertory included the complete oeuvre of Tchaikovsky. His bowing, fingerings and performance suggestions are integral part of this edition by Heifetz's protégé and accomplished violinist in his own right, Endre Granat. Contents: *Andante Funebre, Op. 30 • Humoresque, Op. 10/2 • Méditation, Op. 42/1 • Melody, Op. 42/3 • Scherzo, Op. 42/2 • Sérénade Mélancolique, Op. 26 • Valse-Scherzo, Op. 34*

BAZZINI LA RONDE DES LUTINS (DANCE OF THE GOBLINS) CRITICAL URTEXT EDITION ed. Endre Granat • This great bravura piece uses many of the innovations the composer learned from his teacher, Niccolo Paganini--ricochet and flying staccato bowings, double harmonics, left hand pizzicato, and repetition of the same pitch on all four strings. This work remained one of Jascha Heifetz' favorite encores. He recorded it in 1917 and again in 1937. His bowings, fingerings and his suggestions regarding interpretation are integral part of this edition. HL00153335—S511025

HANDEL PASSACAGLIA FOR TWO VIOLINS ed. Stephen Shipps/ Endre Granat • Outside of his native Norway, Johan Halvorsen (1864-1935) is known internationally only for his arrangement of Handel's *Harpsichord Suite*. The *Passacaglia* is performed as a mainstay of Duo programs, established in the standard literature by playing and recording countless performances with William Primrose and Gregor Piatigorsky. HL00126549—S512002

THE JASCHA HEIFETZ BEETHOVEN FOLIO ed. Endre Granat • Contains Heifetz' Three Cadenzas to the Beethoven *Concerto for Violin and Orchestra in D Major op.61*, along with the Beethoven violin solo with piano works, *Turkish March op. 113* and *Chorus of the Dervishes op.113*, both from *The Ruins on Athens*. All works in the collection are Critical Editions by Endre Granat. HL00145437—S511024

PAGANINI WITCHES DANCE (LE STREGHE) FOR VIOLIN AND PIANO OP. 8, CRITICAL URTEXT EDITION ed. Endre Granat • A mature work of Paganini, *Witches Dance* uses all the innovations he had introduced as a violin virtuoso performer. Like so many of his other works, it was not published during the composer's lifetime. Jascha Heifetz' bowings, fingerings and performance notes are an integral part of this edition. HL00153336—S511026

SAINT-SAËNS INTRODUCTION AND RONDO CAPRICCIOSO ed. Endre Granat • This work was originally intended to be the rousing Finale to Saint-Saëns' *First Violin Concerto, op.20*. Saint-Saëns' favorite violinist Pablo de Sarasate gave the first performance in 1867 in Paris with the composer conducting. In 1869 Saint-Saëns entrusted his younger colleague Georges Bizet to create a reduction of the orchestra score for Violin and Piano. The composer's autograph score and the first edition of the work were the primary source material for this publication. HL00141931—S511021

SAINT-SAËNS HAVANAISE, OP. 83 ed. Endre Granat • The composer dedicated this work which dates from 1885-87 to Rafael Diaz Albertini, a violinist of Cuban origin. This Critical Edition is based on the composer's manuscript, the first print of the violin and piano version, and to a large part, on the historic recording by the composer himself with the violinist Gabriel Willaume (1919). HL00141932—S511012

WIENIAWSKI POLONAISE BRILLANTE NO. 1 (*Polonaise de Concert*) ed. Endre Granat • In 1848, the thirteen year old Henryk Wieniawski wrote the first sketches to his *Polonaise in D Major*. Tremendously popular already during the composer's life time, this work has been on the repertory of virtually every virtuoso violinist ever since. This new edition corrects obvious misprints while keeping the format of the 1853 first edition, printing the textural changes on the Paris version as foot notes. HL00141930—S511020

WIENIAWSKI POLONAISE BRILLANTE NO. 2 ed. Endre Granat • Completed at the zenith of Wieniawski's career in 1869, this virtuoso piece showcases the playing of many fast, short and accented notes on one bow stroke which came to be called the "Wieniawski staccato". The slow midsection in F major contains some of Wieniawski's most lyrical themes while double stops and trills conclude this irresistible work. The signed and dated (1869) manuscript found its home in the library of Jascha Heifetz. As a member of Mr. Heifetz's studio, editor Endre Granat studied this work with the Master. This Critical Edition is based on this manuscript and the first printed edition (Schott 1875). HL00126550—S511019

THE HEIFETZ SCALE BOOK

"Useful and concise... complete scale book for advanced violinists"
—Amazon review

For the first time ever, the HEIFETZ SCALE BOOK presents all the great master violinist Jascha Heifetz' scale routines that were developed over his long career, but never written down! This edition by Heifetz protégé and world-class violinist Endre Granat is a self-contained master class for a lifetime of study in virtuoso technique. The method is systematically presented in twelve units, one for each note in the chromatic scale. HL00172780

Celebrating 100 Years of JASCHA HEIFETZ

PAGANINI 24 CAPRICES

Urtext Edition
Edited by Endre Granat

Since their first publication, Paganini's *Caprices* have been sources of inspiration for many great violinists and composers. Now nearly two centuries later, this publication finally unites a newly-engraved Urtext violin part edited by Endre Granat with expert bowings and fingerings as practiced and taught by legendary violinist and Granat's mentor, Jascha Heifetz. The 2017 release date pays tribute to the master's brilliant 1917 American debut recital at Carnegie Hall. HL00253517

KEISER®

EXCLUSIVELY DISTRIBUTED BY

HAL•LEONARD®

ORDER TODAY from your favorite retailer, or through

halleonard.com